ADULT

PUZZLE

BOOK

As part of this product you have also received FREE access to online tests that will help you to pass Puzzles and Brain Teasers.

To gain access, simply go to:

www.MyEducationalTests.co.uk

Get more products for passing any test at:

www.How2Become.com

Orders: Please contact How2Become Ltd, Suite 14, 50 Churchill Square Business Centre, Kings Hill, Kent ME19 4YU.

You can order through Amazon.co.uk under ISBN: 9781911259886, via the website www.How2Become.com or through Gardners.com.

ISBN: 9781911259886

First published in 2017 by How2Become Ltd.

Typeset by Katie Noakes for How2Become Ltd.

Disclaimer

Every effort has been made to ensure that the information contained within this guide is accurate at the time of publication. How2Become Ltd is not responsible for anyone failing any part of any selection process as a result of the information contained within this guide. How2Become Ltd and their authors cannot accept any responsibility for any errors or omissions within this guide, however caused. No responsibility for loss or damage occasioned by any person acting, or refraining from action, as a result of the material in this publication can be accepted by How2Become Ltd.

The information within this guide does not represent the views of any third party service or organisation.

CONTENTS

6 BENEFITS OF PUZZLE SOLVING

Hello, and welcome to your Adult Puzzle Book. If you are looking for a mentally stimulating and challenging series of exercises, then you have purchased the right product! From ridiculous riddles to complex crosswords, wicked wordsearches to marvellous maths, this book has it all.

Before we get started, let's have a quick look at the key benefits of completing puzzles:

1. MENTAL STIMULATION

Puzzles are a great way to keep your mind mentally active and healthy. Puzzles help your mind to engage in a situation that requires a great deal of thought, concentration, and patience.

It is often argued that keeping your mind active allows you to feel more physically active. Keeping your mind active also allows you to reduce stress levels and reduce fatigue.

2. PUZZLES INSPIRE EDUCATION

One of the benefits of puzzle solving for adults is that it enhances skills such as:

- Research;

- Critical Thinking;

- Cognitive Ability;

- Concentration.

When working out a puzzle, whether that be a crossword or a Sudoku, logical reasoning needs to be applied. Therefore, not only are these puzzles created for your entertainment; they are also educational!

3. RELAXATION

Along with keeping our brains active and healthy, puzzles also help us to relax. Solving puzzles puts your mind in a trance-like-state; which in turn reduces stress levels, increases productivity, and ultimately improves self-confidence.

4. IMPROVING IQ

One of the most valuable benefits of puzzle solving for adults is that it helps to boost your IQ level. In conjunction with this, puzzle solving also improves general knowledge, cognitive skills, memory and problem-solving ability.

5. IMPROVES COGNITIVE ABILITY

Puzzles are fantastic for improving visual performance. Children are able to improve their cognitive ability through recognition of shapes and colours. For adults, cognitive ability goes beyond the basics of recognition of patterns, and allows for more advanced reasoning.

6. CONCENTRATION

The final benefit of puzzle solving for adults, is that puzzle solving improves your concentration skills. Puzzles often require you to think analytically, and therefore increase both the attention span and patience of the puzzle taker. The better your concentration skills, the less mistakes you will make. This is extremely useful for everyday activities.

Now that we've covered the benefits of solving puzzles, let's get started with some brain teasers! There are a total of 100 puzzles in this guide, all of which are designed to push your brain to its limits.

So, with that being said – good luck, and get "cracking!"

PUZZLES 1 - 25

1. UNDER THE SEA

```
W  A  L  G  E  R  A  Y  S  W  H  A  L  E  L
E  S  E  A  W  E  E  D  E  A  W  S  O  I  F
E  A  I  P  L  M  J  W  N  O  C  T  O  S  B
D  C  U  T  L  E  E  S  I  L  P  O  H  E  S
S  R  V  U  D  F  L  D  R  E  E  A  S  A  F
E  A  N  R  Q  S  L  Y  A  S  R  S  I  H  E
A  B  T  T  Z  F  Y  L  M  K  L  A  R  O  C
U  E  T  L  B  J  F  G  B  E  D  G  F  R  S
R  L  R  E  U  O  I  B  U  E  F  J  F  S  G
G  A  F  I  S  H  S  G  S  O  V  L  A  E  I
C  H  D  G  I  P  H  Q  G  G  N  G  E  H  S
S  T  I  N  G  R  A  Y  S  D  E  I  S  D  G
A  B  V  D  R  M  G  A  S  U  P  O  T  C  O
P  N  E  A  G  L  A  F  H  B  A  T  E  R  S
L  Y  R  S  Y  P  O  M  F  C  A  R  B  P  N
```

ALGAE	FISH	SHARK
CORAL	JELLYFISH	STINGRAY
CRAB	OCTOPUS	SUBMARINE
DIVER	SEAHORSE	TURTLE
EEL	SEAWEED	WHALE

2. CELL BLOCKS

Divide the grid into blocks. Each block must be a rectangle or square, and must contain the number of cells indicated by the number.

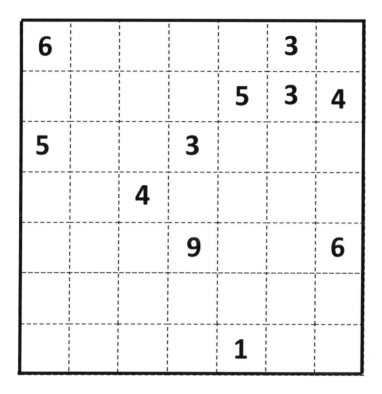

3. RIDDLE

If you give me food, I shall live.

But give me water, and I will die.

What am I?

4. MISSING NUMBERS

Fill in the missing cells so that each row and column contain the numbers 1 to 5.

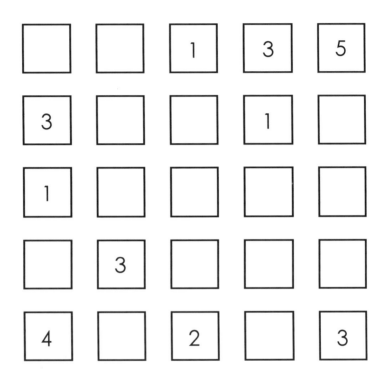

5. RIDDLE

You can hear me but, you can't see me.

I won't speak back until I'm spoken to.

What am I?

6. MISSING LETTERS

Using the letters below, put these in the empty spaces in the grid to form words.

R G I C E M A T R T T M C B U O A T R E E P D N U

P		R	F	E		T		L		E
										N
		A	I		T					
										E
			N	I	C			H		R
F	I	N			R			T		
				B	E			E	R	
	W							R		
U						B				
						A		T		
E			R	A		E	D			

7. BONES

```
E  R  H  K  P  H  A  L  A  N  G  E  S  L  J
B  R  T  H  S  U  R  E  M  U  H  S  F  F  I
C  M  I  T  R  S  A  F  E  M  D  D  I  L  I
M  B  B  B  V  H  Y  L  S  L  S  U  B  I  L
U  A  I  U  S  E  A  E  U  P  L  B  U  A  I
N  B  A  B  S  L  D  L  H  P  T  R  L  S  U
R  D  K  U  L  A  M  I  R  I  A  B  A  X  M
E  Z  P  E  H  J  Y  U  P  C  T  C  A  I  G
T  K  T  G  U  O  M  B  I  O  H  C  S  R  R
S  A  T  K  B  E  C  T  R  N  W  I  M  V  A
P  A  R  E  F  M  E  T  A  D  A  P  H  K  D
P  L  U  B  M  G  R  E  E  J  L  R  N  B  I
K  I  Y  C  M  E  L  C  I  V  A  L  C  O  U
O  Y  H  U  Y  T  C  N  P  A  J  T  J  M  S
E  L  B  I  D  N  A  M  C  H  D  A  N  L  U
```

CLAVICLE	ILIUM	RIBS
CRANIUM	MANDIBLE	SCAPULA
FEMUR	PATELLA	STERNUM
FIBULA	PHALANGES	TIBIA
HUMERUS	RADIUS	ULNA

8. WORD FILL

Place all of the words in the correct position in the grid.

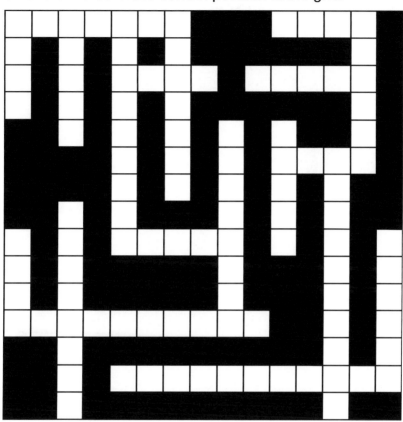

4 LETTERS	Blaze	Monster	Victimised
Love	Drier	**8 LETTERS**	**11 LETTERS**
None	Enter	Abnormal	Objectively
Fire	**6 LETTERS**	Intruder	
Drum	Poetry	**9 LETTERS**	
Iris	Middle	Densified	
5 LETTERS	**7 LETTERS**	**10 LETTERS**	
Blind	Freedom	Squeezable	

9. RIDDLE

When you have me, you want to share me.

When you share me, you no longer have me.

What am I?

10. MISSING NUMBERS

Fill in the missing cells so that each row and column contain the numbers 1 to 5.

	5		2	4
5			4	
	1	5		
	4			
3				5

11. CROSS NUMBERS

Work out the calculations and then write the answers in the correct position on the grid.

	1	2	3		4	5		
6		7			8			9
10	11			12				
13			14				15	
		16		17				
18								19
20				21	22			
		23					24	
	25				26			

ACROSS

1. 15 x 35
4. 72 - 18
7. 6 x 7
8. 6,579 - 84
10. 800 + 58
12. 84 + 240
13. 5 + 50
14. 4 x 5
15. 10 x 7
17. 500 x 4
18. 987 + 653
20. 7 x 5
21. 86 x 2
23. 3,431 - 2,200
24. 17 + 5
25. 40 + 35
26. 317 - 32

DOWN

2. 2 x 124
3. 104 ÷ 2
4. 600 - 38
5. 222 + 222
6. 416 - 31
9. 25 x 20
11. 11 x 5
12. 500 - 198
15. 140 ÷ 2
16. 6 x 9
18. 12 x 11
19. 150 - 18
21. 23 - 10
22. 903 - 191
23. 75 ÷ 5
24. 5 x 5

12. CELL BLOCKS

Divide the grid into blocks. Each block must be a rectangle or square, and must contain the number of cells indicated by the number.

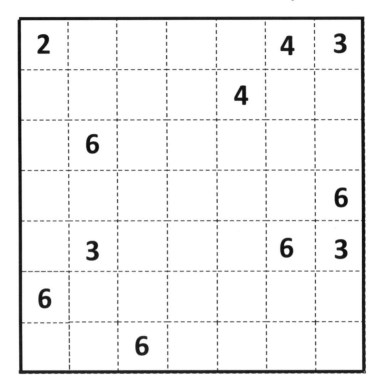

13. RIDDLE

I am a five letter word. Take away the first letter and I sound the same. Take away the last letter and I still sound the same.

What word am I?

14. CROSSWORD

ACROSS

1. What hangs on the wall, has hands and a face, but is not alive?

3. The more there is, the less you will see.

4. Number of fielded players per team in a football match.

6. What type of cheese is made backwards?

DOWN

1. I'm tall when I am young, and get shorter as I get older. What am I?

2. What number will you get if you multiplied all the numbers on a telephone keypad?

5. What starts with 'T', is filled with 'T', and ends with 'T'?

15. SUDOKU

Insert the numbers one to nine into the grid, making sure that every number appears once every in each horizontal and vertical line, and every square (indicated in bold).

9	1		5	6				3
	7		1					9
5				3		1	6	
8		9	7					4
	4				1		9	
	5				3	7		
	3	7		1				5
2					5		3	
1				2	4		7	

16. RIDDLE

What is yours but everybody else uses more?

17. MINI CROSSWORD

1	2	3	4
5			
6			
7			

ACROSS

1. Scrambled or fried

5. To help solve a mystery

6. Dig a _____

7. Night time birds

DOWN

1. Reflected sound

2. Luminous aura

3. Bird of the beach

4. Present tense of the verb 'to see'

18. WONDERS OF THE WORLD

```
P  I  S  A  S  T  O  N  E  H  E  N  G  E  S
V  E  I  S  F  F  P  N  G  E  R  V  U  O  L
T  O  W  E  R  O  F  P  I  S  A  G  H  V  E
N  M  J  I  L  A  H  A  M  J  A  T  H  I  R
O  C  A  F  U  S  T  H  G  U  O  N  S  C  O
Y  J  H  F  R  V  H  L  E  H  P  O  L  T  M
N  M  U  E  S  S  O  L  O  C  E  T  L  O  H
A  T  W  L  E  J  F  A  R  C  R  R  A  R  S
C  O  E  T  G  H  J  S  F  I  A  E  F  I  U
D  E  R  O  K  L  P  Y  Y  P  H  D  A  A  R
N  A  F  W  A  R  G  I  B  U  O  A  R  F  T
A  L  N  E  B  G  I  B  M  H  U  M  G  A  N
R  L  U  R  K  L  R  G  J  C  S  E  A  L  U
G  S  J  A  V  E  F  F  S  A  E  T  I  L  O
T  A  W  R  O  K  G  N  A  M  M  O  N  S  M
```

ANGKOR WAT	LOUVRE	OPERA HOUSE
BIG BEN	MACHU PICCHU	STONEHENGE
COLOSSEUM	MOUNT RUSHMORE	TAJ MAHAL
EIFFEL TOWER		TOWER OF PISA
GRAND CANYON	NIAGRA FALLS	VICTORIA FALLS
	NOTRE DAME	

19. MISSING NUMBERS

Fill in the missing cells so that each row and column contain the numbers 1 to 5.

1		3		
	4			2
		1		
			3	4

20. RIDDLE

You are standing in the middle of an abandoned cabin. In the cabin, there is a lamp, a candle, a fireplace, wood, and some old books. You have one match in your pocket.

Which should you light first?

21. WORD FILL

3 LETTERS	Zebra	7 LETTERS	9 LETTERS
Tin	Lapse	Factory	Blemishes
Tea	Earth	Educate	Harmonica
4 LETTERS	**6 LETTERS**	Stagger	**11 LETTERS**
Grab	Agenda	Genetic	Frequencies
Nest	Abator	Reissue	**12 LETTERS**
Tree	Prince	**8 LETTERS**	Apprehension
5 LETTERS	Outset	Balloons	
Reefs	Bleach		

22. SUDOKU

	2		3			4		
9				1				
4		8		7		5		3
			6			9		7
			1	5	7			
		5			2			
2		4				6		5
				2				8
	1	6	7		8			

23. RIDDLE

What can you hold without ever having to touch it?

24. CODEWORDS

The grid (codeword puzzle):

24			4				25		25	18	6	19	16
18	23	4		18	15	17		12		18		18	
15			2				17		11		17		21
11	18	17	16	11		16		12	1	16		24	2
		18		16		4		23					19
18	11	20	16	15	17	12	23	16		18	22	25	12	19
		16									19		
		23		2	15	25	3	23	4	18	17	2	3	15
	2	15	15				3				14		3
17				10	12	14		18		17		24	
18		18						9		16		17	
8	16	15	14	12	2	15		24	16	13			1
		2								17	23	12	4	8
5	3	4	6	2	16	1							7
		16					26	12	18	23	23	7	

Key:

1	2	3	4	5	6	7	8	9	10	11	12	13
	I										U	

14	15	16	17	18	19	20	21	22	23	24	25	26
		E		A				W		H		

25. ALL ABOUT FOOD

```
L  P  J  M  F  I  P  N  X  J  E  K  R  L  M
D  P  A  S  Y  E  L  O  R  E  S  S  A  C  S
A  N  E  P  E  U  L  N  F  K  P  T  H  A  N
E  I  S  A  I  S  B  M  Y  N  X  E  W  P  A
R  I  E  A  P  Z  O  O  D  O  L  G  E  S  E
B  P  E  I  L  O  Z  J  H  O  Y  G  N  P  B
U  O  H  G  I  C  C  A  T  D  A  U  G  R  D
I  C  C  V  K  D  O  S  B  L  S  N  W  W  E
L  F  I  N  U  T  T  E  F  E  Z  N  F  H  K
B  U  R  G  E  R  S  A  S  S  X  E  O  V  A
S  O  E  N  U  I  N  F  G  A  P  K  L  E  B
X  G  T  H  Z  C  G  O  O  T  P  C  P  E  J
W  C  G  C  Z  E  G  O  F  S  U  I  E  A  D
C  O  G  E  A  T  P  D  W  A  R  H  E  E  H
Y  P  D  H  L  H  E  Y  I  P  C  C  A  I  G
```

BAKED BEANS	CHICKEN NUGGETS	PIE
BREAD	CHIPS	PIZZA
BURGER	EGGS	RICE
CASSEROLE	NOODLES	SEAFOOD
CHEESE	PASTA	YOGHURTS

ANSWERS TO PUZZLES
1 - 25

1. UNDER THE SEA

```
W  A  L  G  E  R  A  Y  S  W  H  A  L  E  L
E  S  E  A  W  E  E  D  E  A  W  S  O  I  F
E  A  I  P  L  M  J  W  N  O  C  T  O  S  B
D  C  U  T  L  E  E  S  I  L  P  O  H  E  S
S  R  V  U  D  F  L  D  R  E  E  A  S  A  F
E  A  N  R  Q  S  L  Y  A  S  R  S  I  H  E
A  B  T  T  Z  F  Y  L  M  K  L  A  R  O  C
U  E  T  L  B  J  F  G  B  E  D  G  F  R  S
R  L  R  E  U  O  I  B  U  E  F  J  F  S  G
G  A  F  I  S  H  S  G  S  O  V  L  A  E  I
C  H  D  G  I  P  H  Q  G  G  N  G  E  H  S
S  T  I  N  G  R  A  Y  S  D  E  I  S  D  G
A  B  V  D  R  M  G  A  S  U  P  O  T  C  O
P  N  E  A  G  L  A  F  H  B  A  T  E  R  S
L  Y  R  S  Y  P  O  M  F  C  A  R  B  P  N
```

2. CELL BLOCKS

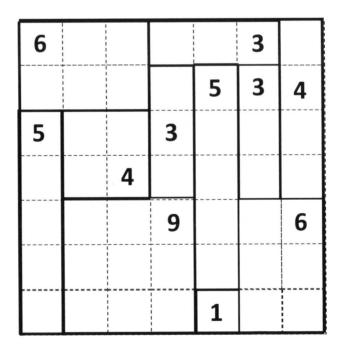

3. RIDDLE

FIRE

4. MISSING NUMBERS

2	4	1	3	5
3	2	5	1	4
1	5	3	4	2
5	3	4	2	1
4	1	2	5	3

5. RIDDLE

ECHO

6. MISSING LETTERS

7. BONES

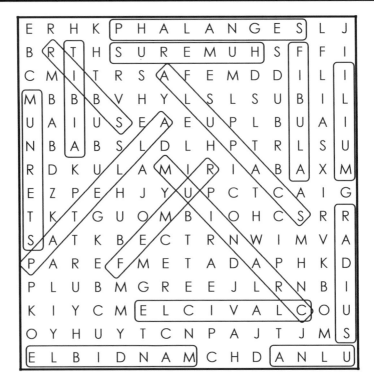

8. WORD FILL

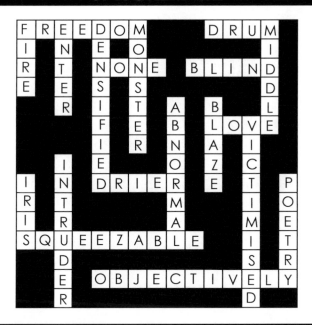

9. RIDDLE

SECRET

10. MISSING NUMBERS

1	5	3	2	4
5	3	2	4	1
4	1	5	3	2
2	4	1	5	3
3	2	4	1	5

11. CROSS NUMBERS

	¹5	²2	³5		⁴5	⁵4	
⁶3		⁷4	2		⁸6	4	9	⁹5
¹⁰8	¹¹5	8		¹²3	2	4		0
¹³5	5		¹⁴2	0			¹⁵7	0
	¹⁶5		¹⁷2	0	0	0	
¹⁸1	6	4	0				¹⁹1
²⁰3	5		²¹1	²²7	2		3
2		²³1	2	3	1		²⁴2	2
	²⁵7	5			²2	8	5	

12. CELL BLOCKS

2					4	3
			4			
	6					
						6
	3			6	3
6					
	6				

13. RIDDLE

EMPTY

14. CROSSWORD

15. SUDOKU

9	1	2	5	6	7	8	4	3
3	7	6	1	4	8	2	5	9
5	8	4	9	3	2	1	6	7
8	2	9	7	5	6	3	1	4
7	4	3	2	8	1	5	9	6
6	5	1	4	9	3	7	8	2
4	3	7	8	1	9	6	2	5
2	9	8	6	7	5	4	3	1
1	6	5	3	2	4	9	7	8

16. RIDDLE

YOUR NAME

17. MINI CROSSWORD

¹E	²G	³G	⁴S
⁵C	L	U	E
⁶H	O	L	E
⁷O	W	L	S

18. WONDERS OF THE WORLD

```
P  I  S  A  S  T  O  N  E  H  E  N  G  E  S
V  E  I  S  F  F  P  N  G  E  R  V  U  O  L
T  O  W  E  R  O  F  P  I  S  A  G  H  V  E
N  M  J  I  L  A  H  A  M  J  A  T  H  I  R
O  C  A  F  U  S  T  H  G  U  O  N  S  C  O
Y  J  H  F  R  V  H  L  E  H  P  O  L  T  M
N  M  U  E  S  S  O  L  O  C  E  T  L  O  H
A  T  W  L  E  J  F  A  R  C  R  R  A  R  S
C  O  E  T  G  H  J  S  F  I  A  E  F  I  U
D  E  R  O  K  L  P  Y  Y  P  H  D  A  A  R
N  A  F  W  A  R  G  I  B  U  O  A  R  F  T
A  L  N  E  B  G  I  B  M  H  U  M  G  A  N
R  L  U  R  K  L  R  G  J  C  S  E  A  L  U
G  S  J  A  V  E  F  F  S  A  E  T  I  L  O
T  A  W  R  O  K  G  N  A  M  M  O  N  S  M
```

19. MISSING NUMBERS

1	2	3	4	5
2	3	4	5	1
3	4	5	1	2
4	5	1	2	3
5	1	2	3	4

20. RIDDLE

MATCH

21. WORD FILL

22. SUDOKU

7	2	1	3	6	5	4	8	9
9	5	3	8	1	4	7	2	6
4	6	8	2	7	9	5	1	3
1	4	2	6	8	3	9	5	7
8	3	9	1	5	7	2	6	4
6	7	5	4	9	2	8	3	1
2	8	4	9	3	1	6	7	5
3	9	7	5	2	6	1	4	8
5	1	6	7	4	8	3	9	2

23. RIDDLE

BREATH

24. CODEWORDS

1	2	3	4	5	6	7	8	9	10	11	12	13
S	**I**	**O**	**M**	**Z**	**B**	**Y**	**P**	**C**	**J**	**D**	**U**	**X**

14	15	16	17	18	19	20	21	22	23	24	25	26
G	**N**	**E**	**T**	**A**	**L**	**V**	**K**	**W**	**R**	**H**	**F**	**Q**

25. ALL ABOUT FOOD

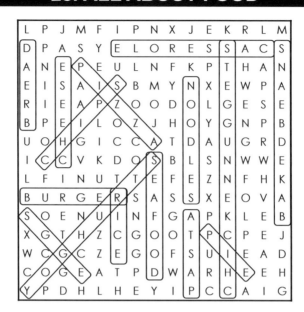

PUZZLES 26 - 50

26. SUDOKU

2						8	3		5
1					6				
9	6			7		2			
	5	7	6					1	
				2					
		2			1			9	7
		1		6				5	3
			3						8
4		3	5					2	6

27. RIDDLE

I have 6 faces but not one body. I have 21 eyes in total, yet cannot see.

What am I?

28. CELL BLOCKS

Divide the grid into blocks. Each block must be a rectangle or square, and must contain the number of cells indicated by the number.

5						1
2			6			
		4		3		
	6					
			2		4	2
2		3				
		5			4	

29. RIDDLE

I have an eye but cannot see; I have a bee without honey; I have a tea without coffee; and a sea without any water.

What am I?

30. MINI CROSSWORD

1		2		3
	■		■	
4				
	■		■	
5				

ACROSS

1. Pirate symbol

4. Narrow; candle

5. Medical professional

DOWN

1. Glossy fabric

2. The hand to have

3. T-shirt size

31. RIDDLE

I am not a river but am full of water. I'm not a plane but I can fly.

What am I?

32. STAR SIGNS

```
R E C N A C L O H E O A U I R
C A N L P H L A S P I O H L I
G I H P I T A L M Y T R I B C
M S E C S I P L I P L B E O A
G M I N I D L B D L R P E I P
S E E G L I O C A A P E G G R
C G G O I P R O C S O C G Y I
T S U R U A T L Q A B R N N C
S H J K L Q Q I L U A A I H O
U T N J M S A U U O I E N L R
R E C T E Q Q G A G U F I O N
U C R I M T N N Q R S M M D O
I S R X Z I S V H I I I E W E
P A U X J Y W B N V S U G M L
S U I R A T T I G A S G S W D
```

AQUARIUS	GEMINI	SAGITTARIUS
ARIES	LEO	SCORPIO
CANCER	LIBRA	TAURUS
CAPRICORN	PISCES	VIRGO

33. MATHS CONUNDRUM

Can you work out these mathmatical conundrums?

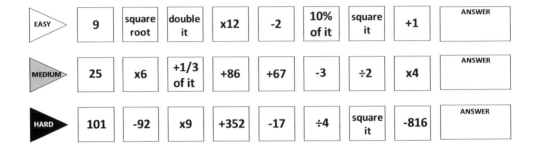

| EASY | 9 | square root | double it | x12 | -2 | 10% of it | square it | +1 | ANSWER |

| MEDIUM | 25 | x6 | +1/3 of it | +86 | +67 | -3 | ÷2 | x4 | ANSWER |

| HARD | 101 | -92 | x9 | +352 | -17 | ÷4 | square it | -816 | ANSWER |

34. MISSING NUMBERS

Fill in the missing cells so that each row and column contain the numbers 1 to 5.

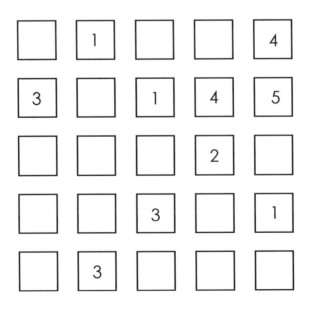

	1			4
3		1	4	5
			2	
		3		1
	3			

35. WORD FILL

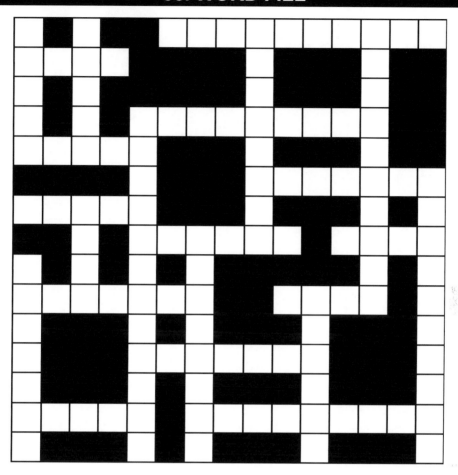

4 LETTERS	Grief	Rattles	Necklaces
Roll	Alien	Midterm	**10 LETTERS**
Pair	Upset	Amateur	Consummate
Iced	**6 LETTERS**	**8 LETTERS**	Reciprocal
Acre	Negate	Ignorant	Narcissism
5 LETTERS	Castle	Gemstone	**12 LETTERS**
Fungi	**7 LETTERS**	**9 LETTERS**	Disintegrate
Alibi	Abdomen	Daffodils	

36. SUDOKU

8	1	5					3	
	3		9					
4		6		3				
6				1				
	5		3		8		7	
		9		4				1
				2		3		8
					9		2	
	7					5		4

37. RIDDLE

I am always in front but never behind.

What am I?

38. MYTHICAL CREATURES

```
G  M  I  N  I  O  D  F  L  P  C  L  O  P  S
P  E  G  A  S  U  S  N  N  I  E  M  D  Y  U
G  G  U  J  Y  M  G  R  N  L  N  E  I  P  P
R  R  B  V  U  K  O  Y  T  I  T  G  A  T  I
F  I  T  E  Y  C  A  Y  C  E  A  O  M  N  R
A  F  A  F  I  I  C  N  R  B  U  L  R  T  S
P  F  S  N  S  B  L  O  E  I  R  L  E  A  U
K  I  U  F  B  L  E  E  S  G  A  S  M  S  H
B  N  D  F  K  I  L  R  N  F  D  F  E  P  B
U  R  E  I  O  B  G  O  G  O  U  L  M  O  W
E  E  M  Z  B  Z  H  W  R  O  A  L  V  L  I
F  G  D  R  A  G  O  N  D  T  S  I  Z  C  W
O  A  T  I  Z  G  G  I  A  N  T  O  Q  Y  B
O  S  E  K  W  U  Q  L  P  I  G  N  G  C  Z
G  Y  T  M  K  W  U  R  U  A  T  O  N  I  M
```

BIGFOOT	GIANT	OGRE
CENTAUR	GRIFFIN	PEGASUS
CYCLOPS	MEDUSA	TROLLS
DRAGON	MERMAID	UNICORN
FAIRY	MINOTAUR	YETI

39. VOWELLESS PUZZLE

As you can see, all the vowels have been removed from the puzzle. Complete the grid by adding the vowels A, E, I, O or U in the correct place.

40. RIDDLE

I have married many people, but never been married.

Who am I?

41. CELL BLOCKS

Divide the grid into blocks. Each block must be a rectangle or square, and must contain the number of cells indicated by the number.

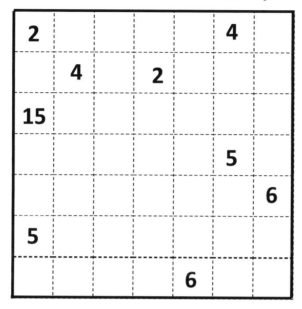

42. FONT SCRAMBLE

Unscramble the different fonts and work out the names of each famous person.

a **a a** a *a a* b c **d** *d* d c e e e e *h* i I i i I I **I m** m m

m *m* n n n *n* o o 0 o p r r r s s s s t t t t t u w y

43. COUNTRIES OF THE WORLD

```
I  R  E  L  A  N  D  B  B  Z  I  A  R  L  M
D  G  E  N  P  O  R  R  E  S  C  P  A  I  N
N  L  U  L  I  Z  A  R  B  X  Y  E  E  N  N
A  M  E  A  O  C  A  U  O  D  P  S  R  T  E
L  A  L  C  I  A  C  C  H  N  R  N  O  A  W
R  B  A  I  E  N  I  L  A  A  U  I  P  L  Z
E  A  Q  T  B  X  T  B  A  L  S  Z  A  A  E
Z  N  Z  G  E  A  R  Z  A  G  S  A  G  N  A
T  E  B  M  I  E  R  N  S  N  I  D  N  D  L
I  W  T  S  B  D  I  O  E  E  I  N  I  E  A
W  Z  S  O  L  H  S  P  B  G  A  A  S  V  N
S  U  U  E  C  N  A  R  F  L  B  D  P  N  D
R  Y  N  A  C  I  R  F  A  H  T  U  O  S  O
S  O  U  T  H  K  L  C  A  N  A  D  A  N  L
T  A  G  J  E  B  A  I  L  A  R  T  S  U  A
```

AUSTRALIA	ENGLAND	RUSSIA
BRAZIL	FRANCE	SINGAPORE
CANADA	IRELAND	SOUTH AFRICA
CHINA	MEXICO	SPAIN
CYPRUS	NEW ZEALAND	SWITZERLAND

44. SUDOKU

			1	2	3	8		
8	3		6				1	2
		1			4			
5		8	4			9		3
	9				6		8	
1		4				6		5
			3			5		
4	5				8		9	1
			7	4	5			

45. RIDDLE

I have keys, but no lock. I have a space, but no room. I have a window, but no door.

What am I?

46. MISSING NUMBERS

Fill in the missing cells so that each row and column contain the numbers 1 to 5.

47. CELL BLOCKS

Divide the grid into blocks. Each block will be a rectangle and square, and must contain the number of cells indicated by the number.

				2		4
			8			
5	2			2	1	2
					1	
		4		3		
	4		5	6		

48. ASTRONOMY

```
P  L  M  C  O  T  E  N  A  L  P  B  R  O  G
F  A  L  O  X  Y  C  E  L  P  Y  K  D  K  M
C  D  Q  N  S  F  Y  B  A  G  X  G  Z  U  L
O  A  R  S  H  D  H  U  W  I  A  W  Z  Y  R
N  R  F  T  A  I  X  L  Q  U  L  A  T  A  E
E  K  T  E  M  O  C  A  Z  X  A  R  A  C  P
T  M  M  L  P  R  G  A  L  A  G  H  L  C  P
I  A  O  L  H  E  A  R  T  H  Y  U  S  G  I
L  T  Y  A  L  T  O  C  H  M  S  J  T  N  D
L  T  B  T  E  S  T  H  R  T  J  K  A  S  G
E  E  B  I  A  A  F  A  E  O  H  G  R  E  I
T  R  M  O  O  N  A  R  R  O  N  N  S  L  B
A  V  S  N  H  B  K  D  X  W  L  U  S  L  E
S  B  T  S  G  N  R  A  D  J  N  H  M  A  H
E  F  F  A  L  L  O  O  I  M  O  I  I  T  T
```

ASTEROID	EARTH	PLANET
CLUSTER	GALAXY	SATELLITE
COMET	MOON	STAR
CONSTELLATION	NEBULA	SUN
DARK MATTER	ORB	THE BIG DIPPER

49. COLOUR CODED NUMBERS

Place the numbers 1 to 9 in the 9 x 9 grid. The number in the circle should equal the sum of the four surrounding squares. The numbers in each colour need to add up to the number shown beneath the grid.

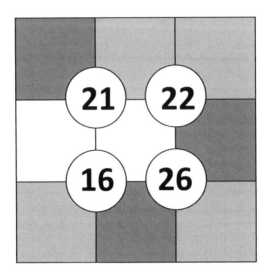

50. RIDDLE

What do these words have in common?

Level   Racecar   Refer   Madam   Kayak

ANSWERS TO PUZZLES
26 - 50

26. SUDOKU

2	7	4	1	9	8	3	6	5
1	3	8	2	5	6	7	4	9
9	6	5	4	7	3	2	8	1
3	5	7	6	4	9	8	1	2
8	1	9	7	2	5	6	3	4
6	4	2	8	3	1	5	9	7
7	8	1	9	6	2	4	5	3
5	2	6	3	1	4	9	7	8
4	9	3	5	8	7	1	2	6

27. RIDDLE

A DICE

28. CELL BLOCKS

29. RIDDLE

THE ALPHABET

30. MINI CROSSWORD

¹S	K	²U	L	³L
A	■	P	■	A
⁴T	A	P	E	R
I	■	E	■	G
⁵N	U	R	S	E

31. RIDDLE

CLOUD

32. STAR SIGNS

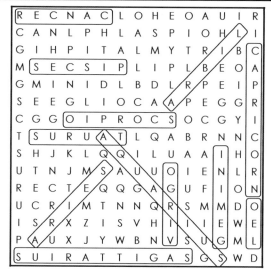

33. MATHS CONUNDRUM

EASY = 50

MEDIUM = 700

HARD = 10,000

34. MISSING NUMBERS

5	1	2	3	4
3	2	1	4	5
1	5	4	2	3
2	4	3	5	1
4	3	5	1	2

35. WORD FILL

36. SUDOKU

8	1	5	6	7	4	2	3	9
7	3	2	9	5	1	4	8	6
4	9	6	8	3	2	7	1	5
6	8	7	2	1	5	9	4	3
1	5	4	3	9	8	6	7	2
3	2	9	7	4	6	8	5	1
9	4	1	5	2	7	3	6	8
5	6	3	4	8	9	1	2	7
2	7	8	1	6	3	5	9	4

37. RIDDLE

TOMORROW

38. MYTHICAL CREATURES

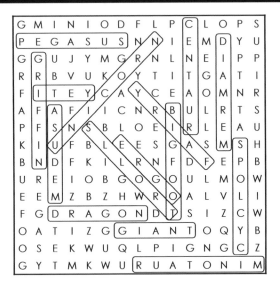

39. VOWELLESS PUZZLE

40. RIDDLE

A PRIEST

41. CELL BLOCKS

2				4	
	4	2			
15					
				5	
					6
5					
			6		

42. FONT SCRAMBLE

Will Smith **(MV Boli font)**

Tom Cruise **(Juice ITC font)**

Madonna **(Impact font)**

Britney Spears **(Bradley Hand ITC font)**

Matt Damon **(Lucida Handwriting font)**

Adele **(Microsoft Himalaya)**

43. COUNTRIES OF THE WORLD

```
I R E L A N D B B Z I A R L M
D G E N P O R R E S C P A I N
N L U L I Z A R B X Y E E N N
A M E A O C A U O D P S R T E
L A L C I A C C H N R N O A W
R B A I E N I L A A U I P L Z
E A Q T B X T B A L S Z A A E
Z N Z G E A R Z A G S A G N A
T E B M I E R N S N I D N D L
I W T S B D I O E E N I E A
W Z S O L H S P B G A A S V N
S U U E C N A R F L B D P N D
R Y N A C I R F A H T U O S O
S O U T H K L C A N A D A N L
T A G J E B A I L A R T S U A
```

44. SUDOKU

7	4	5	1	2	3	8	6	9
8	3	9	6	5	7	4	1	2
6	2	1	9	8	4	3	5	7
5	6	8	4	1	2	9	7	3
3	9	2	5	7	6	1	8	4
1	7	4	8	3	9	6	2	5
2	8	7	3	9	1	5	4	6
4	5	3	2	6	8	7	9	1
9	1	6	7	4	5	2	3	8

45. RIDDLE

COMPUTER KEYBOARD

46. MISSING NUMBERS

3	2	1	4	5
2	4	5	1	3
1	5	3	2	4
5	1	4	3	2
4	3	2	5	1

47. CELL BLOCKS

				2		4
			8			
5	2			2	1	2
					1	
		4		3		
	4		5	6		

48. ASTRONOMY

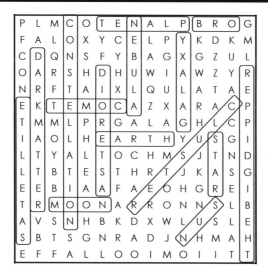

49. COLOUR CODED NUMBERS

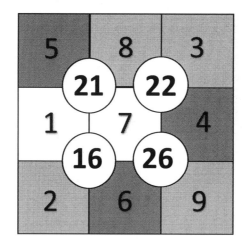

50. RIDDLE

PALINDROME WORDS

PUZZLES 51 - 75

51. CODEWORDS

2		26		22		21		12	5	13	6	14
5		16		13		15					15	
13	5	16	13		5	13	24	12	26		20	5
17			12	13	5				13		13	5
			16		13			25	16	11	3	16	17
26					6		13		2		16		6
11	13	25	1	6	14	16	2					12
13			2				10					15
2		24	1	23			9	13	25	2	4	13	5	14
16			15				12		10		10	
			12	13	19	26		22	5	13	4	22	9	16
	15			24		13			26			
13	22	15	5	12		2	10	14	16		8	10	1	18
	16			16		9			5			1
3	7	11	16	5		7		6	7	6	9	1	26	12

1	2	3	4	5	6	7	8	9	10	11	12	13
				R	C						T	

14	15	16	17	18	19	20	21	22	23	24	25	26
K		E										S

52. ANIMALS IN THE WILD

For this word search, the below words have been muddled up. Unscramble the words, and then find them in the word search.

```
O  X  Y  S  U  M  A  T  O  P  O  P  P  I  H
W  R  T  F  F  E  L  T  M  O  N  P  C  S  K
Z  E  B  R  A  G  N  P  T  K  Y  R  E  L  A
C  H  E  K  B  A  B  L  U  B  O  L  P  I  S
V  S  X  Z  H  Z  Q  M  B  C  O  L  B  O  S
G  T  L  P  V  K  U  L  O  A  P  E  M  N  U
D  M  E  R  I  P  M  D  S  L  Y  O  I  N  R
P  L  Y  H  O  N  I  S  L  O  T  P  P  H  E
E  L  O  M  L  L  A  N  E  Y  H  A  V  H  C
F  G  L  E  E  C  K  P  E  E  O  R  E  A  O
F  O  A  L  W  A  O  H  O  G  N  D  Y  T  N
A  R  F  A  M  K  R  T  Y  B  K  H  X  E  I
R  F  F  D  Y  M  Y  E  K  N  O  M  N  E  H
I  D  U  A  S  F  X  F  F  E  F  L  Y  H  R
G  X  B  Z  W  A  R  T  H  O  G  L  L  C  E
```

FFLAOBU	MPOTAHIOUPPS	YLXN
HEACHTE	YNHAE	YPHNTO
OECRILCDO	DAELROP	HORIESNUCRO
NPALHETE	ILNO	GAOTRHW
ERGAIFF	ENMKOY	AEBRZ

53. CELL BLOCKS

Divide the grid into blocks. Each block must be a rectangle or square, and must contain the number of cells indicated by the number.

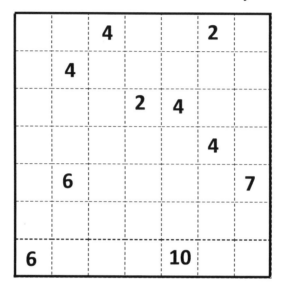

54. MISSING NUMBERS

Fill in the missing cells so that each row and column contain the numbers 1 to 5.

55. ANAGRAM CONUNDRUM

Solve the eight-letter anagram.

B	A	D	S	E	T	U	P

56. MINI CROSSWORD

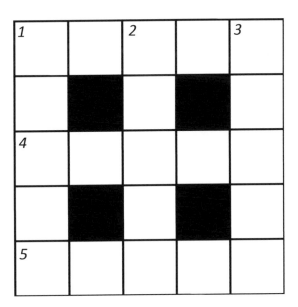

ACROSS

1. Age measurements

4. Family relation

5. Monopoly purchase

DOWN

1. Younger generation

2. English racecourse

3. Crustacean's protection

57. THE ROMANS

For this word search, the below words have been muddled up. Unscramble the words, and then find them in the word search.

```
L  T  T  O  I  R  A  H  C  L  O  H  X  J  E
L  E  K  R  H  C  S  L  A  T  I  N  C  S  F
G  E  G  E  S  A  E  G  G  Y  S  S  O  N  G
L  S  G  M  X  R  A  F  K  S  X  H  H  H  B
D  E  R  S  I  S  E  N  A  T  O  R  T  T  Q
A  N  O  P  E  W  S  I  O  A  O  A  C  A  K
O  L  A  K  D  U  L  I  D  C  U  C  J  K  B
R  U  D  Z  L  C  E  O  B  L  D  C  C  V  O
S  S  S  U  R  V  G  L  O  E  O  R  A  C  U
M  N  M  U  E  L  E  G  I  O  N  S  E  B  D
O  O  S  H  M  I  R  D  E  R  S  U  S  O  I
R  C  N  T  C  U  D  E  U  Q  A  M  A  U  C
M  T  O  R  O  R  E  P  M  E  A  E  R  C  C
Q  O  C  J  P  L  H  R  E  M  S  R  T  X  A
A  G  L  A  D  I  A  T  O  R  S  O  C  I  L
```

QEUCTDUA	SULCON	SUREM
THSBA	RORPEEM	DSROA
ACCUDIBO	ARSDTOGLIA	UROMLUS
CAREAS	INLAT	SAEORNT
IOARCHT	GIOLENS	DISOERLS

58. ARROWORD

Work out the words from the description, and write them in the direction the arrow is pointing.

Loathed; scorned	Consumer Savings account ▼	⤵		Dishonest	⤵		Modify to fit	⤵
⤷								
					--, myself, and I ▼	Pop the question ▼		
	⤴			Depicts geography ▶				
				Chess piece ▼				
Archery weapon ▼	Body part	Burning flames ▼						
						Pool of water ▼		
⤴							Fluorescent colours	
Church activity					Antonym; off ▶		▼	
Clear spirit	⤵		Type of tree ▶					
Heaven; messenger								
⤷								

59. ANAGRAM CONUNDRUM

Solve the eight-letter anagram.

P	E	S	H	I	S	E	H

60. ONE TO NINE

Using the numbers 1 to 9 (only once), complete the grid in order for the calculations to be correct.

	+		+	7	= 12
X		X		X	
3	X		-		= 25
X		X		+	
	+		-	8	= 3
=		=		=	
15		216		22	

61. ALPHABET SUDOKU

Using the letters A to I, complete the sudoku so that each row and column contains all these letters. Each 3 x 3 grid must also contain the letters A to I.

I			H				A	D
	F							
	E	A		C		I		G
G	D			F		E	B	
					E		G	
	A	B		G				
D		G		B		F	H	
							E	
F	B				D			A

62. RIDDLE

What can travel the world, but remain in a corner?

63. MISSING NUMBERS

Fill in the missing cells so that each row and column contain the numbers 1 to 5.

3	2			
	4			1
		5		
	5			
4			1	

64. ONE TO NINE

Using the numbers 1 to 9 (only once), complete the grid in order for the calculations to be correct.

9	**X**		**-**	**2**	**= 25**
X		**+**		**+**	
	+	**1**	**X**		**= 32**
X		**X**		**X**	
	-		**X**		**= 18**
=		**=**		**=**	
504		**20**		**36**	

65. GREEK MYTHOLOGY

```
A  R  T  S  T  H  E  F  A  T  E  S  F  A  T
P  L  Z  H  M  H  E  S  A  A  A  C  H  I  L
A  R  E  H  M  L  E  G  D  S  T  O  D  S  S
H  S  U  T  F  T  E  M  Q  F  F  H  W  G  A
E  U  S  L  L  E  Z  S  U  L  H  V  E  D  L
S  T  F  A  N  S  N  Z  E  S  L  F  R  N  T
E  S  U  S  A  A  E  S  T  J  E  M  L  S  A
M  E  S  T  T  E  S  E  I  G  Y  S  U  O  S
R  A  H  I  I  M  A  S  D  S  B  O  G  L  A
E  H  T  D  T  E  T  S  O  N  A  K  S  E  E
H  P  Y  A  Y  D  A  E  R  A  I  D  E  A  D
P  E  S  D  O  G  E  D  H  T  Y  T  Z  U  H
H  H  M  U  T  S  S  D  P  S  H  T  Y  M  G
H  A  D  E  S  D  E  O  A  T  P  M  G  Y  K
A  P  H  R  O  I  H  G  S  I  M  E  T  R  A
```

APHRODITE	GODS	MYTHS
ARTEMIS	HADES	THE FATES
ATHENA	HEPHAESTUS	THE MUSES
ATLAS	HERA	TITANS
GODDESSES	HERMES	ZEUS

66. WORD FILL

3 LETTERS	Knee	Zebra	Exposer
Big	Walk	Cream	**8 LETTERS**
Sew	Omit	Zests	Lathered
Egg	Lime	Allow	**9 LETTERS**
4 LETTERS	**5 LETTERS**	**6 LETTERS**	Addiction
Plot	Safer	Indeed	Lawnmower
Sour	Blame	Bumper	Treasures
Tame	Ratio	**7 LETTERS**	**12 LETTERS**
Ugly	Haste	Psyched	Professional

67. COLOUR CODED NUMBERS

Place the numbers 1 to 9 in the 9 x 9 grid. The number in the circle should equal the sum of the four surrounding squares. The numbers in each colour need to add up to the number shown beneath the grid.

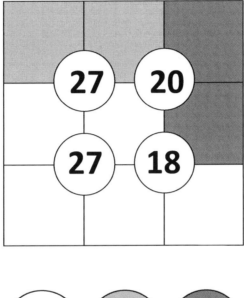

68. BRAIN TEASER

How many times does the letter 'a' appear in the numbers 0 to 100?

69. ALPHABET SUDOKU

Using the letters A to I, complete the sudoku so that each row and column contains all these letters. Each 3 x 3 grid must also contain the letters A to I.

	A			D		B		
	E				I			F
B			E					A
			C		D	G		B
		E			A		C	
D	C						A	
		B		C			H	D
		I		F		E	B	
H			D		B			

70. RIDDLE

What wears a cap but has no head?

71. BOGGLE

Can you find 15 words using the below letters in 5 minutes? Letters can be used in any combination but must be vertically, horizontally or diagonally adjacent.

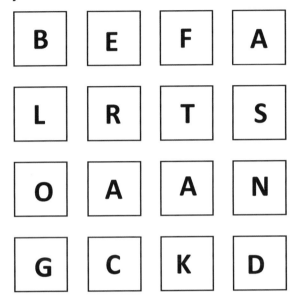

B	E	F	A
L	R	T	S
O	A	A	N
G	C	K	D

72. MISSING NUMBERS

Fill in the missing cells so that each row and column contain the numbers 1 to 5.

2				
	2			3
3		2		
		5	4	
	5			1

73. DINOSAURS

```
A D S U R U A S O I H C A R B
S I O P O A D V E O P R V A T
S P S T S I C T R P L R E S S
U L D U I D P T R E A G L U E
R O I S R W O D I P S M O R S
U D L A T U A P E J T K C U P
A O O U E D A F O L E F I A O
S C X R S V I S R R G D R S T
O U Y U A B J V O O E W A O A
H S N S Q I U V A N A H P G R
P T O C L F G B G F N W T E E
O B Y V M S N I D S A A O T C
L K R S A U R O P O D A R S I
I F A N O D O N A U G I H Y R
D W B S U R U A S O N I P S T
```

BARYONYX	IGUANODON	THEROPODS
BRACHIOSAURUS	SAUROPODA	TRICERATOPS
DILOPHOSAURUS	SPINOSAURUS	TYRANNOSAURUS
DIPLODOCUS	STEGOSAURUS	VELOCIRAPTOR

74. ONE TO NINE

Using the numbers 1 to 9 (only once), complete the grid in order for the calculations to be correct.

	+	5	-	4	= 9
-		x		x	
	+		+		= 6
-		x		x	
	x	7	x		= 378

=	=	=
1	70	108

75. ANAGRAM CONUNDRUM

Solve the eight-letter anagram.

C	Y	R	T	I	N	U	S

ANSWERS TO PUZZLES
51 - 75

51. CODEWORDS

1	2	3	4	5	6	7	8	9	10	11	12	13
I	D	H	M	R	C	Y	Q	L	U	P	T	A

14	15	16	17	18	19	20	21	22	23	24	25	26
K	O	E	W	Z	G	V	J	B	X	F	N	S

52. ANIMALS IN THE WILD

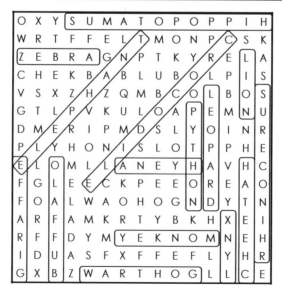

53. CELL BLOCKS

		4		2	
	4				
			2	4	
				4	
	6				7
6				10	

54. MISSING NUMBERS

4	1	3	5	2
5	2	1	3	4
3	5	4	2	1
1	3	2	4	5
2	4	5	1	3

55. ANAGRAM CONUNDRUM

B	A	D	S	E	T	U	P
B	U	D	A	P	E	S	T

56. MINI CROSSWORD

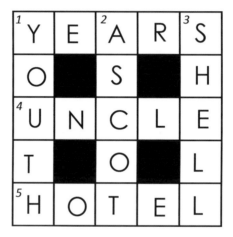

¹Y	E	²A	R	³S
O		S		H
⁴U	N	C	L	E
T		O		L
⁵H	O	T	E	L

57. THE ROMANS

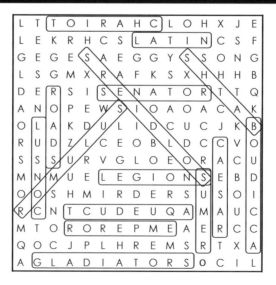

58. ARROWORD

Loathed; scorned	Consumer / Savings account	U	Dishonest	L	■	Modify to fit	A
D	I	S	L	I	K	E	D
■	S	E	■	E	--, myself, and I	Pop the question	A
■	A	R	M	Depicts geography / Chess piece	M	A	P
Archery weapon	Body part	Burning flames	■	B	E	S	T
B	■	F	■	I	■	K	■
O	■	I	■	S	■	Pool of water	
W	O	R	S	H	I	P	Fluorescent colours
Church activity	■	E	■	O	Antonym; off	O	N
Clear spirit	G	■	Type of tree	P	I	N	E
Heaven; messenger	I	■	■	■	■	D	O
A	N	G	E	L	■	■	N

59. ANAGRAM CONUNDRUM

P	E	S	H	I	S	E	H
S	H	E	E	P	I	S	H

60. ONE TO NINE

1	+	4	+	7	= 12
x		x		x	
3	x	9	-	2	= 25
x		x		+	
5	+	6	-	8	= 3

=	=	=
15	216	22

61. ALPHABET SUDOKU

I	G	C	H	E	F	B	A	D
B	F	D	G	A	I	H	C	E
H	E	A	D	C	B	I	F	G
G	D	I	A	F	C	E	B	H
C	H	F	B	D	E	A	G	I
E	A	B	I	G	H	C	D	F
D	I	G	E	B	A	F	H	C
A	C	H	F	I	G	D	E	B
F	B	E	C	H	D	G	I	A

62. RIDDLE

A STAMP

63. MISSING NUMBERS

3	2	1	5	4
5	4	3	2	1
2	1	5	4	3
1	5	4	3	2
4	3	2	1	5

64. ONE TO NINE

9	x	3	-	2	= 25
x		+		+	
7	+	1	x	4	= 32
x		x		x	
8	-	5	x	6	= 18
=		=		=	
504		20		36	

65. GREEK MYTHOLOGY

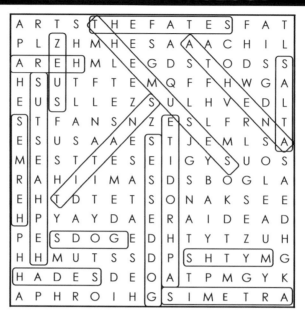

66. WORD FILL

67. COLOUR CODED NUMBERS

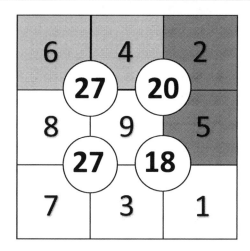

68. BRAIN TEASER

ZERO

69. ALPHABET SUDOKU

F	A	H	G	D	C	B	I	E
G	E	C	B	A	I	H	D	F
B	I	D	E	H	F	C	G	A
A	H	F	C	I	D	G	E	B
I	B	E	F	G	A	D	C	H
D	C	G	H	B	E	F	A	I
E	F	B	I	C	G	A	H	D
C	D	I	A	F	H	E	B	G
H	G	A	D	E	B	I	F	C

70. RIDDLE

A BOTTLE

71. BOGGLE

AT, AS, GO, BE, AN, OR, FAT, SAT, TAN, RAT, CAR, AND, LOG, RAN, BET, TAR, CAT, TAG, LET, ARE, ART, CAN, BRA, COG, ERA, FRO, LAG, OAK, OAR, OAT, ORB, LEFT, ROCK, BLOG, RACK, GOAL, SAND, FAST, COL, CAST, DARE, FATE, CORE, RATS, GORE, SAFE, CANS, LOCK, ROLE, CARE, NACK, GOAT, CATS, OATS, STAR, DATA, BRAT, TANK, TACK, BETS, SAKE, GALE, CORE, FROG, DART, CART, LACK, BRAN, BETA, BRAG, COAT, GATE, FEREL, STAND, TRACK, CORAL, BLOAT, DARTS, STALE, SNACK, STARE, FATAL, BLARE, SNARE, STACK, BLOCK, AFTER, BRAND, CARTS, BLACK, COATS, GOATS, FROCK, GATER, CARAT, CAROL, STRAND, LOCATE, FASTER, REBLOG, STALER, CARATS.

You may have even found a word not on this list, if so well done!

72. MISSING NUMBERS

2	4	1	3	5
5	2	4	1	3
3	1	2	5	4
1	3	5	4	2
4	5	3	2	1

73. DINOSAURS

```
A  D  S  U  R  U  A  S  O  I  H  C  A  R  B
S  I  O  P  O  A  D  V  E  O  P  R  V  A  T
S  P  S  T  S  I  C  T  R  P  L  R  E  S  S
U  L  D  U  I  D  P  T  R  E  A  G  L  U  E
R  O  I  S  R  W  O  D  I  P  S  M  O  R  S
U  D  L  A  T  U  A  P  E  J  T  K  C  U  P
A  O  O  U  E  D  A  F  O  L  E  F  I  A  O
S  C  X  R  S  V  I  S  R  R  G  D  R  S  T
O  U  Y  U  A  B  J  V  O  O  E  W  A  O  A
H  S  N  S  Q  I  U  V  A  N  A  H  P  G  R
P  T  O  C  L  F  G  B  G  F  N  W  T  E  E
O  B  Y  V  M  S  N  I  D  S  A  A  O  T  C
L  K  R  S  A  U  R  O  P  O  D  A  R  S  I
I  F  A  N  O  D  O  N  A  U  G  I  H  Y  R
D  W  B  S  U  R  U  A  S  O  N  I  P  S  T
```

74. ONE TO NINE

8	+	5	-	4	= 9
-		x		x
1	+	2	+	3	= 6
-		x		x
6	x	7	x	9	= 378

=   =   =
1   70   108

75. ANAGRAM CONUNDRUM

C	Y	R	T	I	N	U	S
S	C	R	U	T	I	N	Y

PUZZLES 76 - 100

76. CROSS NUMBERS

Work out the calculations and then write the answers in the correct position on the grid.

	1	2			3			
	4			5				6
7		8				9	10	
	11			12	13		14	
	15				16			
17				18				19
		20				21		
	22			23	24			
	25				26			

ACROSS

1. 978 - 354
3. 1180 ÷ 2
4. 50 - 9
5. 8 + 9
8. 1,000 - 668
9. 444 ÷ 4
12. 41 x 2
14. 5 x 5
15. 509 - 141
16. 103 + 388
17. 5 + 42
18. 100 ÷ 10
20. 2,530 ÷ 5
21. 85 + 306
22. 87 - 28
23. 5 x 182
25. 800 - 585
26. 658 - 82

DOWN

1. 8^2
2. 74 + 139
3. 96 - 39
5. 896 ÷ 7
6. 1,030 ÷ 2
7. 21 + 76
10. 11^2
11. 1,000 -163
13. 5 x 48
17. 5 x 9
18. 397 - 228
19. 487 + 231
20. 900 - 309
21. 784 - 477
22. 468 ÷ 9
24. 8 + 7

77. VOWELLESS PUZZLE

As you can see, all the vowels have been removed from the puzzle. Complete the grid by adding the vowels A, E, I, O or U in the correct place.

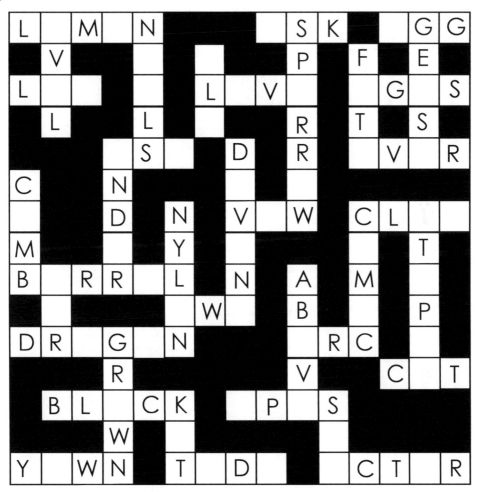

78. RIDDLE

Your mother's brother's only brother-in-law is having a bbq.

Who is having the bbq?

79. CROSSWORD

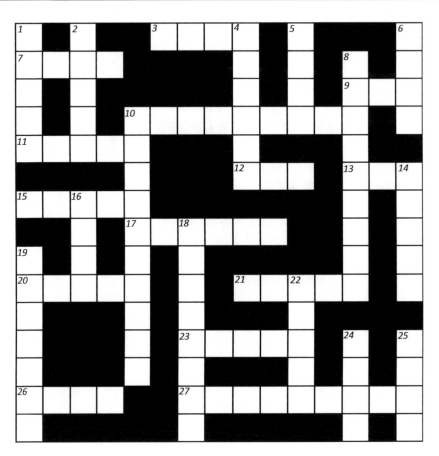

ACROSS

3. "Swear under _____" (4)

7. Water related (4)

9. Ciao! (3)

10. Vigorous supporters of a cause (9)

11. From another planet (5)

12. Nothing on the scoreboard (3)

13. Immoral offence (3)

15. Thin, transparent fabric (5)

17. Summon with gesture (6)

20. Tree knot (5)

21. Careless error (5)

23. Desert water spot (5)

26. Bouncing sound (4)

27. Compulsory system (9)

DOWN

1. Hot dance; hot sauce (5)	**16.** Arm bone (4)
2. _____ bar (5)	**18.** Redacted; hidden from view (8)
4. Beyond the pearly gates (6)	**19.** Failed to consider (7)
5. What an old-fashioned romantic does while courting (4)	**22.** "Hasta la _____" (5)
6. Royal Navy woman (4)	**24.** Trap of food (4)
8. Unable to let go (9)	**25.** Hill; sand (4)
10. Second wife to Henry VIII (4,6)	
14. Mythological maiden (5)	

80. MISSING NUMBERS

Fill in the missing cells so that each row and column contain the numbers 1 to 5.

	4			2
5			4	
		4		
			5	
	1	3		5

81. HABITATS OF ANIMALS

```
P  I  N  F  U  M  Q  T  N  A  I  M  U  L  P
S  E  V  I  H  I  O  N  U  A  Q  M  I  N  O
E  S  A  S  T  B  L  A  S  P  N  D  O  S  N
B  E  I  R  D  I  L  E  A  C  A  Q  S  A  D
U  U  U  E  T  R  M  C  O  B  W  E  B  S  K
S  R  R  Q  A  H  I  O  G  A  L  V  P  U  B
S  R  K  R  A  U  P  N  B  B  L  C  N  Y  U
M  O  B  O  O  S  N  O  A  S  H  O  L  E  T
U  D  W  Y  F  W  E  T  V  E  L  Q  L  N  D
I  C  H  K  J  S  S  P  H  N  P  J  D  M  J
R  I  U  J  T  U  T  K  E  N  N  E  L  S  V
A  O  L  S  L  G  J  O  E  V  E  J  A  L  M
U  Q  E  D  O  A  Y  I  N  C  T  Y  I  A  Q
Q  N  Q  S  N  D  I  Y  A  O  J  C  R  Q  P
A  Q  U  A  E  B  H  E  V  A  C  N  Q  A  D
```

AQUARIUMS	DEN	LAIR
BURROWS	EARTH	NESTS
CAVE	HIVES	OCEAN
COBWEBS	HOLE	POND
COOPS	KENNELS	STABLES

82. MISSING LETTERS

Using the letters below, put these in the empty spaces in the grid to form words.

N S B R H M P N G I K C P L R S O R E S N D

A C A H A

T		E		E					H	Y
A						E				
	R	O		R	E				A	
						C		A		C
C				O						
A		T			E	R		Y		
		A		E		T				L
A			O	Y	S			S		D
B		K			H		Y			
		S			E		E			E
E						E		I	G	

83. SUDOKU

					6		5	8
	5	7			9	2	4	
9	6							
		3	9				6	
6				4				2
	2				3	4		7
							3	1
	1		8	7		5	2	
7	9			5				

84. CRACK THE CODE

Can you work out what the code is saying?

CODE:
WRKAT IEPUN CHEDJ ACOBA NDMAD EHISN OSEBL EEDUI

85. ANAGRAM CONUNDRUM

Solve the eight-letter anagram.

B	U	S	T	R	O	C	T

86. COLOUR CODED NUMBERS

Place the numbers 1 to 9 in the 9 x 9 grid. The number in the circle should equal the sum of the four surrounding squares. The numbers in each colour need to add up to the number shown beneath the grid.

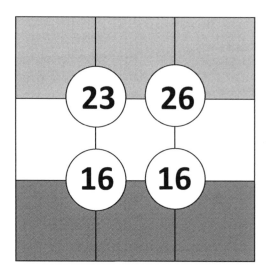

87. CROCO PUZZLE

For each puzzle, you will need to fill in the grid so that each row/column adds up to the total (indicated by the block above or to the left of it).

The numbers 1 – 9 can only be used once in each sum. For example, if you are working out the total for '8', you cannot use two 4s.

The same digit may occur more than once in a row or column, so long as it is used only once to work out each vertical and horizontal total.

The grid contains the following clue numbers:

Top row clues: 16, 21, 24, 25, 9, 11, 23

Left/down clues within grid: 13, 15, 25, 6, 12, 15, 19, 15, 16, 31, 8, 4, 10, 15, 17, 14, 7, 1, 2, 12, 8, 12, 29, 11, 20, 8

88. ARROWORD

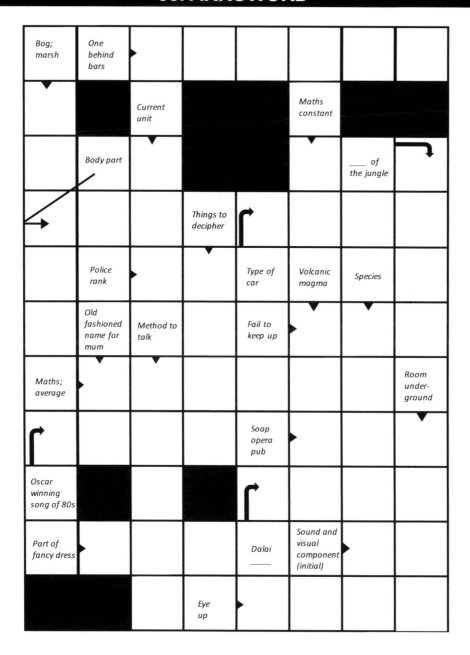

89. CRACK THE CODE

Can you work out what the code is saying?

CODE:

PENST HEREA REMAN YUNFO RTUNA TEMYT HSABO UTABR AHAML INCOL NCATE

90. MATHS CONUNDRUMS

Can you work out these mathematical conundrums?

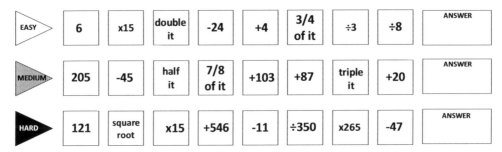

EASY	6	x15	double it	-24	+4	3/4 of it	÷3	÷8	ANSWER
MEDIUM	205	-45	half it	7/8 of it	+103	+87	triple it	+20	ANSWER
HARD	121	square root	x15	+546	-11	÷350	x265	-47	ANSWER

91. ANAGRAM CONUNDRUM

Solve the eight-letter anagram.

D	E	W	C	H	E	R	N

92. VISITING ITALY

```
B O L O G N A G L P H G E L M
F L R J A L J C E P L N A P P
L S A E N T O C P A L I Y I M
E O A C H K N M F R T A S X K
S R N Z C E V J E U O A I O A
V E R N R U C U R S D U E B C
V O I O N A L I M I A N N S L
E R L B E P N R K M F P A E R
N F O V P A L E R M O O R L B
I B L F N O A Q Q A B V L P D
C J I K L M M I O E E S V A H
E L I E A O Z P E F F M S N I
A O C F S O R R E N T O O A O
X J A O N E G W C I U T H R F
U M D F A N O R E V I F N J S
```

BOLOGNA	NAPLES	SIENA
FLORENCE	PALERMO	SORRENTO
GENOA	PISA	TURIN
LUCCA	POMPEII	VENICE
MILAN	ROME	VERONA

93. CROCO PUZZLE

For each puzzle, you will need to fill in the grid so that each row/column adds up to the total (indicated by the block above or to the left of it).

The numbers 1 – 9 can only be used once in each sum. For example, if you are working out the total for '8', you cannot use two 4s.

The same digit may occur more than once in a row or column, so long as it is used only once to work out each vertical and horizontal total.

94. COLOUR CODED NUMBERS

Place the numbers 1 to 9 in the 9 x 9 grid. The number in the circle should equal the sum of the four surrounding squares. The numbers in each colour need to add up to the number shown beneath the grid.

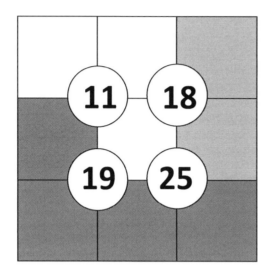

95. ANAGRAM CONUNDRUM

Solve the twelve-letter anagram.

T	O	P	S	T	O	P	R	U	N	I	S

96. SUDOKU

	5		2			6	7	
	9					8	4	
2		3	6					
6					1		5	
5	7				9			4
	1				6			
		7			8			
9	2	5					1	
		8		4				

97. RIDDLE

Trevor works at his local butchers. He is a slim man of 6 feet tall. He wears a size 11 shoe.

What does he weigh?

98. MISSING NUMBERS

Fill in the missing cells so that each row and column contain the numbers 1 to 5.

	2		4	
	5	4		
		3		
1				5
		1	5	

99. ONE TO NINE

Using the numbers 1 to 9 (only once), complete the grid in order for the calculations to be correct.

1	+		-		= 0
+		+		+	
	X	5	X		= 120
X		X		X	
	X	8	-	9	= 47
=		=		=	
35		56		81	

100. WORLD CURRENCIES

```
L P J Y V J D O L L A R D L E
C C L T R G V J L N A D R N J
N E I V A Q V G A I C R A T E
A B R M U J Z Z N G O H R Q N
R H A G J B D S B I L L D V O
F K E D A F F F N O L A D O R
R I A A R C C S R E F R L R K
I B U U L I E U O A A D E F H
L D B E F H E O I L A Q I T V
Q L O L V S P C S L D E R K S
E M R B R V U O E E E L O B C
Q P E B A F R R U R P E S H W
E E U U A V Q A I D I N A R T
Y Z D R L P J V H T N V X G K
H A S H I L L I N G G E E C Z
```

DINAR	KRONE	RUBLE
DOLLAR	LIRA	RUPEE
EURO	PESO	STERLING
FRANC	RIEL	SHILLING

ANSWERS TO PUZZLES
76 - 100

76. CROSS NUMBERS

	1:6	2:2	4		3:5	9	0	
	4:4	1		5:1	7			6:5
7:9		8:3	3	2		9:1	10:1	1
7	11:8		12:8	13:2		14:2	5	
	15:3	6	8		16:4	9	1	
17:4	7		18:1	0			19:7	
5		20:5	0	6		21:3	9	1
	22:5	9		23:9	24:1	0		8
	25:2	1	5		26:5	7	6	

77. VOWELLESS PUZZLE

78. RIDDLE

YOUR FATHER

79. CROSSWORD

¹S		²S		³O	A	T	⁴H		⁵W	⁶W
⁷A	Q	U	A				E		O	⁸O	R
L		S					A		O	⁹B	Y	E
S		H		¹⁰A	C	T	I	V	I	S	T	S	N
¹¹A	L	I	E	N			E			E	
		N				¹²N	I	L		¹³S	I	¹⁴N
¹⁵G	A	¹⁶U	Z	E						S		Y
		L		¹⁷B	E	C	K	O	N	I		M
¹⁹I		N		O			E			V		P
²⁰G	N	A	R	L			²¹B	E	²²V	U	E	H
N		E		S			I				
O		Y		²³O	A	S	I	S		²⁴B		²⁵D
R			N		R				T	A		U
²⁶E	C	H	O			²⁷E	D	U	C	A	T	I	O	N	E
D					D					T	

80. MISSING NUMBERS

1	4	5	3	2
5	3	2	4	1
2	5	4	1	3
3	2	1	5	4
4	1	3	2	5

81. HABITATS OF ANIMALS

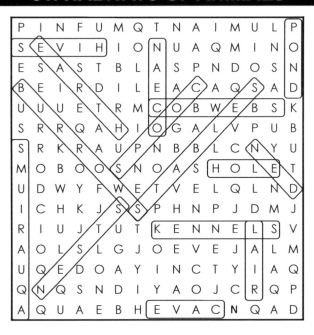

82. MISSING LETTERS

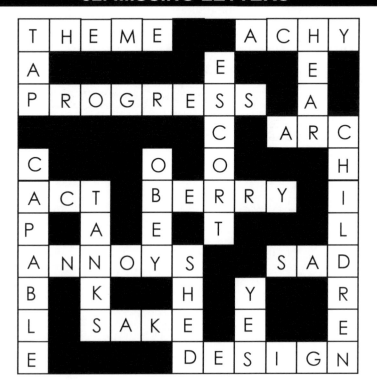

83. SUDOKU

2	3	1	4	6	7	9	5	8
8	5	7	1	3	9	2	4	6
9	6	4	5	2	8	1	7	3
4	7	3	9	1	2	8	6	5
6	8	9	7	4	5	3	1	2
1	2	5	6	8	3	4	9	7
5	4	8	2	9	6	7	3	1
3	1	6	8	7	4	5	2	9
7	9	2	3	5	1	6	8	4

84. CRACK THE CODE

KATIE PUNCHED JACOB AND MADE HIS NOSE BLEED

85. ANAGRAM CONUNDRUM

B	U	S	T	R	O	C	T
O	B	S	T	R	U	C	T

86. COLOUR CODED NUMBERS

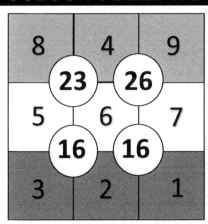

87. CROCO PUZZLE

	16	21		24	25	9		11	23
13	7	6	15	2	5	8	25	1	9
6	4	2	12	8	9	1	5	3	2
15	5	3	2	4	1		9	2	1
19 / 15	5	1	6	7	16	3	5	3	
31	5	4	9	1	3	7	2	8	8
4	3	1	15	3	10 / 17	4	6	14	7
1	1	2 / 8	2	12 / 12	7	5		8	4
29	6	3	7	5	8	11	2	6	3
20		5	6	7	2	8	8		

88. ARROWORD

Bog; marsh	One behind bars	►I	N	M	A	T	E
S	■	Current unit	■		Maths constant	■	
W	Body part	A	■		P	___ of the jungle	K
A	R	M	Things to decipher	M	I	N	I
M	Police rank	►P	C	Type of car	Volcanic magma	Species	N
P	Old fashioned name for mum	Method to talk	O	Fail to keep up	L	A	G
Maths; average	►M	E	D	I	A	N	Room underground
F	A	M	E	Soap opera pub	V	I	C
Oscar winning song of 80s	■	A	■	L	A	M	A
Part of fancy dress	►W	I	G	Dalai ___	Sound and visual component (initial)	A	V
■		L	Eye up	►O	G	L	E

89. CRACK THE CODE

THERE ARE MANY UNFORTUNATE MYTHS ABOUT ABRAHAM LINCOLN

90. MATHS CONUNDRUM

EASY = 5

MEDIUM = 800

HARD = 483

91. ANAGRAM CONUNDRUM

D	E	W	C	H	E	R	N
W	R	E	N	C	H	E	D

92. VISITING ITALY

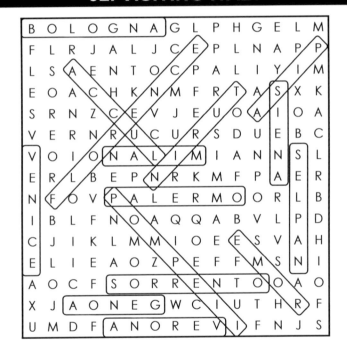

93. CROCO PUZZLE

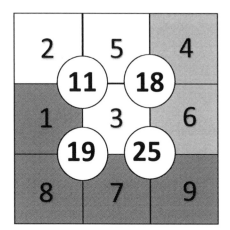

94. COLOUR CODED PUZZLE

95. ANAGRAM CONUNDRUM

T	O	P	S	T	O	P	R	U	N	I	S
O	P	P	O	R	T	U	N	I	S	T	S

96. SUDOKU

8	5	1	2	9	4	6	7	3
7	9	6	3	1	5	8	4	2
2	4	3	6	8	7	5	9	1
6	8	9	4	2	1	3	5	7
5	7	2	8	3	9	1	6	4
3	1	4	5	7	6	2	8	9
4	3	7	1	5	8	9	2	6
9	2	5	7	6	3	4	1	8
1	6	8	9	4	2	7	3	5

97. RIDDLE

MEAT

98. MISSING NUMBERS

3	2	5	4	1
2	5	4	1	3
5	1	3	2	4
1	4	2	3	5
4	3	1	5	2

99. ONE TO NINE

1	+	2	-	3	= 0
+		+		+	
4	x	5	x	6	= 120
x		x		x	
7	x	8	-	9	= 47
=		=		=	
35		56		81	

100. WORLD CURRENCIES

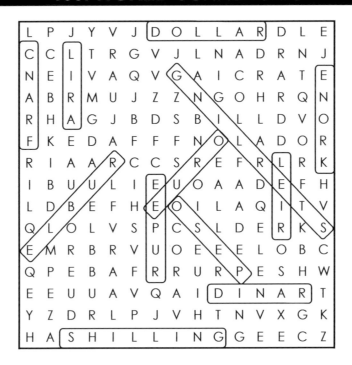

```
L  P  J  Y  V  J  D  O  L  L  A  R  D  L  E
C  C  L  T  R  G  V  J  L  N  A  D  R  N  J
N  E  I  V  A  Q  V  G  A  I  C  R  A  T  E
A  B  R  M  U  J  Z  Z  N  G  O  H  R  Q  N
R  H  A  G  J  B  D  S  B  I  L  L  D  V  O
F  K  E  D  A  F  F  F  N  O  L  A  D  O  R
R  I  A  A  R  C  C  S  R  E  F  R  L  R  K
I  B  U  U  L  I  E  U  O  A  A  D  E  F  H
L  D  B  E  F  H  E  O  I  L  A  Q  I  T  V
Q  L  O  L  V  S  P  C  S  L  D  E  R  K  S
E  M  R  B  R  V  U  O  E  E  E  L  O  B  C
Q  P  E  B  A  F  R  R  U  R  P  E  S  H  W
E  E  U  U  A  V  Q  A  I  D  I  N  A  R  T
Y  Z  D  R  L  P  J  V  H  T  N  V  X  G  K
H  A  S  H  I  L  L  I  N  G  G  E  E  C  Z
```

Get Access To
FREE
Puzzle Resources

www.MyEducationalTests.co.uk

22712561R00075

Printed in Great Britain
by Amazon